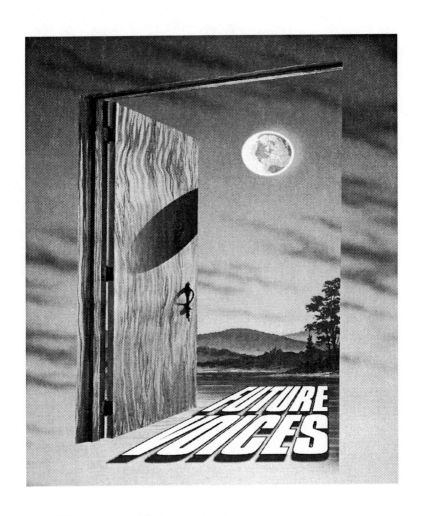

FROM NOTTINGHAMSHIRE
VOL II

Edited by Dave Thomas

First published in Great Britain in 2000 by
YOUNG WRITERS
Remus House,
Coltsfoot Drive,
Woodston,
Peterborough, PE2 9JX
Telephone (01733) 890066

HB ISBN 0 75431 954 7
SB ISBN 0 75431 955 5

FOREWORD

This year, the Young Writers' Future Voices competition proudly presents a showcase of the best poetic talent from over 42,000 up-and-coming writers nationwide.

Successful in continuing our aim of promoting writing and creativity in children, our regional anthologies give a vivid insight into the thoughts, emotions and experiences of today's younger generation, displaying their inventive writing in its originality.

The thought, effort, imagination and hard work put into each poem impressed us all and again the task of editing proved challenging due to the quality of entries received, but was nevertheless enjoyable. We hope you are as pleased as we are with the final selection and that you continue to enjoy *Future Voices From Nottinghamshire Vol II* for many years to come.

CONTENTS

Louise Bryant	31
Russell Phillips	32
Alicia Joyner	33
Amy Perrins	34
Jason Holberry	35
Clare Cowley	36
Hannah Jones	37
Natalie Bowen	38
Leanne Dexter	39
Rachel Beth Groves	40
Sheryl Earnshaw	41
Chris Coyle	42
Michelle North	43
Adele Brown	44
Heather Lloyd	45
Claire Hales	46
Nathan Steen	47
Sophie Bryant	48
Nyssa Walster	49
Shaun Roberts	50
Luke Fagan	51
Michael Etchells	52
James Kimberley	53
Adam Kerley	54

Haywood School

Afia Amin	55
Sophia Rehman	56
Emily Walton	57

King Edward VI School

Jacob Millin	58
Ryan Willows	59
Louise Wilkinson	60
Victoria Wyles	61
Karla Barratt	62
Laura Baker	63
Gemma Burgess	64

The Poems

BLACK

Black is blindness,
Not able to see,
Like a pitch-black night,
Or under a calm, dark sea.

Black is confusion,
Not knowing what's there,
Like a question with no answer,
Or not knowing where.

Black is death,
The finish, the end,
The end of something,
Something you cannot mend.

Robbie Keevil (14)
Belvoir High School

METAPHOR

I am the pro who can
beat everyone,
knife-sharp skills,
No one else can beat
I am as good as I want
to be,
But if I don't try, I can't
focus on me.
Every month, every week
Someone puts me to the test,
But no one can deny that
I am the *best!*

Stuart Freestone (14)
Belvoir High School

GREY

What is grey?
Grey is the peacemaker
Of black and white
Grey is the pigeon
That flies like a kite
Grey is the man
Who's ancient and dying
Grey are the clouds
As they start their crying
Grey is the horse
That's shy and serene
Grey is the beard
Of the old has-been
Grey is the height
Of the elderly and old
Grey is the colour
That you have been told.

Amelia Bolland (14)
Belvoir High School

A TREE

A tree is a family
Each characteristic is a tiny leaf
Each thought they have is a twig
Upon many a branch there is hope.

The love is the trunk
The protective parents are the bark
The chances that go wrong
are fallen leaves.

Each droplet of rain feeds
their hopes and dreams
Each separate twig and
branch are the feelings and
fights they share
The roots are the strong points
which hold them together.

Each leaf that falls is a
mistake to be forgotten
Each fruit that ripens
is happiness and life.

Amy Linday (13)
Belvoir High School

RED

Raging and living
The Black Angel's own weapon
Root of all evil.

Tommy Partridge (13)
Belvoir High School

NO TIME

I'm a prisoner in a cell,
waiting for my trial.
I cannot get out.
The bars are made from hearts,
but there is no time for me.
The judge has no time
for my sentence.
I have plain bread and water,
the others get cakes and wine.
My voice will not be heard by those
who can set me free.

Colleen Gibson (13)
Belvoir High School

A Crow Among Swans

I am a crow among swans,
covered with thick white paint.
I try to fly, but my wings have been clipped;
I am made to swim.
I am a lost child in New York.
I speak, although everything
I say is already wrong.
I play the game, I've already lost
I sing the song, and no one knows the tune.
I open a file, but access is denied . . .

Kimberley Thackeray (13)
Belvoir High School

EMBARRASSMENT!

I've eaten a dry, burning desert,
I've swallowed a pillow of feathers,
I'm a stereo without any speakers,
My mind is a blank piece of paper,
That swells and swells till it is an Arctic wasteland.
My face is a red-hot furnace,
I'm a stone churning in my stomach.
I'm a cat among a group of cats,
And I'm shrinking, sinking, being swallowed by
My shoes.

Holly Bennett (13)
Belvoir High School

METAPHOR POEM

I am a book not yet read,
Whose words no one knows,
I am a name with no identity,
A parrot just repeating,
Saying words meaningless to me,
But above all this,
I am a picture,
Not yet finished.

Naomi Yeandle (13)
Belvoir High School

EASILY READ?

A scarlet rose between two thorns.
Blazing torches though my fire's died out.
A red apple with a rotten core.
Temperamental, I think not.
A red-breasted robin in among the sparrows,
Carries the spirit on its wing.

I am an open book with the first chapter already written,
Caution is not enough, danger looms ahead.
Crowned by my glory, as berries on a tree,
An autumnal flush.

I am the blood of a poppy,
You'll surely remember me.

Laura Hallam (13)
Belvoir High School

BLACKNESS

Devil-black darkness,
Diabolical demons,
Depressing, distressing,
Wicked, wizards.
Witchcraft, threatening,
Furious, villainous,
Gloomy, filthy,
Dirty, evil,

Blackness!

Adam Carr (13)
Belvoir High School

SILVER, SILVER EVERYWHERE

There's silver when the moon does shine,
There's silver when we all do dine,
There's silver in the jewellery box,
There's silver when the front door knocks.

Silver is the ghostly phantom,
That creeps around in a tantrum,
Silver is the white cloud's lining,
That floats about and keeps climbing.

There's silver when bright stars glow,
There's silver when the stream does flow.
There's silver when the moon does shine,
There's silver when we all do dine.

David Hudson (13)
Belvoir High School

NIGHT-TIME

The midnight sky is a dark cold blanket
The cool blue scattered with tiny diamonds
The clouds move like waves towards the horizon.
Its misty whiteness galloping like wild horses
The moon shines like a golden globe
Its sad face watching over the land
The cool night air chills all living things
Whilst in summer there's only a gentle breeze
And as the sun starts to rise
The cool blue softens before your eyes.

Claire Hamer (13)
Belvoir High School

BLUE

Blue is the colour of calm
Then why is it blue for a boy?
There are blue-eyed boys
Not all of them blue-blooded
Not all of them Conservatives.

Blue is the colour of nature and delphiniums
And out of the blue
Blue whales crash their blue bellies against the water
Avoiding blue-green algae
Splashing across blue rock.

Blue is the colour of excellence
University blues line up in blue suits
Blue chip shares are owned by the lucky few
A blue ribbon of honour distinguishes not many
And blu-tack sticks dependably to blue walls.

Blue is the colour of unpleasantness
And smelly English cheese
Blue mould grows hairily on leftovers in the fridge
Pornography is blue
And blue tits make us titter.

Blue is the colour of music and films with Blues Brothers
There are rhapsodies written in blue
To stop you feeling blue
When you've listened to enough *Blue Moon* by Andy Williams
And Eiffel 65.

I like blue
Not navy blue, but sky blue and peacock blue
The blue in Lego bricks and the curtains in the spare bedroom
I like gentle blues and turquoise blues
But I hate feeling blue.

Edward Proctor (13)
Belvoir High School

RAINBOW MAGIC

Red is the colour of a tree full of cherries,
And a bush full of bright red berries.
Orange is the colour of the sun,
Watched by the baker making a bun.
The vibrant colour, yellow,
Is extremely mellow.
Green grass grows,
In the field with noisy crows.
A deep blue is the sea,
Which drowned the little bumblebee.
Indigo is the colour of a brand new car,
Which shines as brightly as the Great North Star.
Violet's the colour of a dark, dismal room,
Which is full of the deepest gloom.
All these colours make up one thing,
The rainbow with the colours that sing.

Sarah Richards (13)
Belvoir High School

WHITE WHISPERS

Like a dream they float us by
Cotton wool faces in the sky.
Purest shade of all the colours
White is the one without any other.

Angel voices sing so sweet
The white robes bow down at heaven's feet.
Crisp winter snow glistens in the day
Clean and fresh it melts away.

White icy footsteps on cold winter days
Jack Frost has been and spread his ways.
The sea has white horses which ride alone
The old scruffy dog has a new shiny bone.

A small white mouse scampers by
His features gleam against his eye.
The eternal flame burns on and on
White is the light when day is gone.

Rachel Lane (13)
Belvoir High School

BUNCHES

The first time
It sped in a candyfloss rush
With all the meaning of milk dissipating
With a swirl of my index stirring
A teabag's grainy memory, floating . . . by

The third time
I had broken from my carriage
To cloak the figure of my mind's eye
The train rattled
A funeral march of myth.

Supine atop a tower yearning upwards,
High as the pupil perceives
This pupil you conceives;
Flanked by walls concrete and four, a
Timber door gasping into thin air.

Downwards collapsing
The sunflowers have eaten their eponymy. The beanstalk
De-petalled and uprooted, is split.
Where concrete meets abortive soil
I lie like lilacs. There is no single entrance.

Clawing walls, I came away with a fistful of
Pebbles.
Clutching tight I dreamt of Rapunzel. Of
Pebbles to rain to hair to form
To conform to legend to cascade to Earth.

Like bark buck teeth a door swung open
A smile swung wide, white as a prince's keep, his
Shadow was black, bolting his hips to his
Finger to its fingers, mouth joined to mouth in
Grinning plurality, from tips to toes.

Lizzie I did it for you
Who pirouettes in black dresses and loathes height so
You who wears hair straight and long enough to climb
Lizzie he has tufts of your hair, I saw
Bunches, bunches, bunches.

Buckling inwards with the blow his unlit shadow
Mimicked falling fading cousins - red, black and blue
You were toppling - like china
You hit the ground, I saw
It was I who was rising.

Ewan Gass (17)
Bilborough College

DREAMS

People and places are all in my dreams,
Sometimes so real (or so it seems).
Floating on air and falling to wake
with a bolt and a quiver that would make you quake.
I've seen figures all twisted and torn,
only to walk at the break of dawn.
If my dreams were to come true one day,
What would I wish for, there's such an array.

Claire Dixon (14)
Bircotes & Harworth Community School

FEELINGS

People all have feelings,
Maybe down deep inside,
But when a person is emotional,
He has no feelings to hide.

Feelings can be nasty,
Feelings can be good,
Whatever you are feeling,
Try and feel good.

Whenever you are down,
And when you're feeling bad,
If people try to help you,
Don't bring them down with you.

So everybody is different,
Their feelings are too,
So don't get on their wrong side,
Or you may end up black and blue.

Nathan Rainey (14)
Bircotes & Harworth Community School

THE SEASONS

Spring is here
buds begin to burst
new life is being born
no more winter storms

Summer is here
people cheer
late summer nights
early morning starts

Autumn is here
leaves begin to fall
colours of gold and brown
this season doesn't make me frown

Winter is here
spring is near
weather is cold and sharp
frosty tree shapes glisten in the dark.

Jody Smith (14)
Bircotes & Harworth Community School

THIS MORNING

This morning my dad shouted
This morning my dad swore
There was water through the ceiling
There was water on the floor
There was water down the stairs
The kitchen stools were floating
So were the dining chairs

This morning I've been crying
Dad made me so upset
He shouted and he swore at me
Just 'cause things got so wet
I only turned the tap on
To get myself a drink
The trouble is I didn't see
The plug was in the sink.

Ryan Millns (14)
Bircotes & Harworth Community School

EXAMS

The month of June is nearly here,
The most stressful time of the year.
It's time to see what you have learnt,
And whether you get the grades you've earnt.

Staying in your room all day,
Hoping that the time will go away.
All you seem to do is revise,
And doing this is what I despise.

My sister keeps driving me up the wall,
Sometimes I feel like hitting her with a cricket ball.
She can be nice sometimes though,
Yeah right! As nice as yellow snow!

A couple of months later you start to sweat,
About what grades you are going to get.
Maybe you will do good,
Or maybe you'll fail,
As long as you try hard it doesn't matter at all.

Andrew Dowse (16)
Bircotes & Harworth Community School

My Sunshine

I love the sun
But then who doesn't?
It's my lifeline, smiling, happy,
Warm.

Sometimes though it gets captured by a cloud
Then I feel sad as it lowers its head,
Blinks out light in momentary flashes
Of less melancholy times.

Soon though, the cloud always lifts
And there it is again
Like the brightest bauble on the Christmas tree
Dancing in its stillness.

I didn't make the cloud move though -
Not this time.
I always try but it never lets me
Get close enough.
I can only witness its weeping.

But then maybe if I do get close to my sun
I'll get burned.
Some things are only meant to be seen from a distance -
My sun is one of them.

Laura Dawson (16)
Elizabethan High School

A RAY OF HOPE

Darkness and chaos;
Folding with fury;
The sky groaned.
Rumbling, rolling, raging,
The doors of hell opened.

The wind whispering
Howling through the trees;
Weeping clouds,
Full of anger and rage
Pelting down like bullets.

Cascading and echoing,
A ray of hope
The last drop descends;
Maybe we will cope.
All's still.

As clear as crystal,
The sky blue ocean
With its heavenly music;
All but a notion
A spectrum of life.

Hayley Cawston (17)
Elizabethan High School

SEA

The sea is calm tonight.
Clear, blue. Glistening in the light of the moon.
Like delight in a child's eye,
Like a bride on her wedding day,
Like a proud father gazing at mother and son.

As dawn breaks clouds shroud the pleasure.
The sea becomes lonely, desperate,
With a longing to reflect light,
Time gone by,
Memories.

I often gaze at the sea,
To let changing emotions wash over me.
It hides my tears.
Comforts my fears.

The salty air haunts me wherever I go, from time to time.
I know I must return,
To the glistening sea, beautiful in the moonlight.
With the knowledge of many men's dreams.
To the sea I must return.

Elizabeth Burkwood (16)
Elizabethan High School

THE ORANGE

The soft strange skin
Like an animal's leather.
Sliced in two the glistening flesh,
The tender fruit squeezed dry,
Acidic fruit left smooth and damp.
Smells sweet as honey,
Fizzing bubbles drip steadily.
Now glowing a finale before the very end.

Lauren Fulcher (14)
Elizabethan High School

THE BOWL

The beautiful cut glass bowl
Stood proud on the centre of the dining table
It is the centre of attraction for displaying fruit
It protects the fruit from bruising
The beautiful glass glistens in the sunlight
The glistening glass brings joy to the eye
Its crystal shines silently
The extreme elegance reminds you of a lady of refinement.

Michelle Hoskins (14)
Elizabethan High School

THE SKY!

The light blue sky surrounds me,
The stillness and the brightness of its control,
Clouds gather like a blanket of cotton wool,
The smell of fresh air haunts me,
A beautiful, blue ocean so peaceful to the ear,
Its new born freshness is smooth yet strong,
Its continuous beauty is like the light of life.

Claire Farnsworth (15)
Elizabethan High School

THE ROSE

The deep red flower is unique from all the rest,
Such an innocent head with a protecting body of thorns.
Swaying swiftly, dancing like a queen,
In charge of all her soldiers marching in green.
She's known for her power and passion,
Yet smells so sweet and gentle.
As soft as silk to touch,
Burning bright like a candle, till daylight turns to dusk.

Lianne Gary (14)
Elizabethan High School

PURPLE PILLOW

The purple pillow sitting on my bed
Quietly it rests
The scent from the heart shape
Wafts up my nose, and around
My bed, soon smelling sweet.
I smell the pillow, every day
It makes me relax
It is patiently, permanently placed,
Sitting still, smelling sweet.

Louise Bryant (14)
Elizabethan High School

HANGING SHIRT

The proud owner stares at the glorious football top
hanging upon the wall.
He thinks about the great and mighty victories and the sad losses.
Every time it is worn it acts like a lucky charm,
like God watching over us all.
As the sun shines through the dark clouds,
the mighty claret and blue brightens up the day.
When the fans cheer the distinguished name,
the players play with more passion than they ever have done before.

Russell Phillips (15)
Elizabethan High School

THE WINDOW

The brilliant white window with the pane of glass
Shimmering in the sun,
So smooth, so shiny, so new,
Was my viewpoint on the bustling world.
The window creaked as it opened
And the curtains danced in the breeze.
The rustling ripped the silence
Like a crack of thunder,
Yet the window was solid and permanent.

Alicia Joyner (14)
Elizabethan High School

THE CANDLE

Standing tall in the window,
Clean and white as snow,
Its burning fragrance fills the room.
The fragile flickering flame sways in the air,
The hot clear wax slowly rolls down the side,
Like a snowball down a hill,
The warm glow from the candle illuminates the room,
A cameo is drawn on the wall,
Then a whisper of wind and the candle is out.

Amy Perrins (14)
Elizabethan High School

THEATRE OF DREAMS

Old Trafford stands tall and true
haunting to visitors,
and welcoming to its proud fans.
Inside the atmosphere is electric,
yet terrifying for the opposing team.
As the players come out the tunnel
the trumpet sounds to mark the start
of a tremendous battle between
twenty-two men and a ball.

Jason Holberry (15)
Elizabethan High School

THE SUN

The sun shines brightly against the pale blue sky and
> cotton wool clouds.

She smiles at the world from her superior position,
Making birds sing tunefully from their perches in the green trees.
The yellow is like a beautiful bright buttercup,
Heating the cool breeze to a warm breath of air.
As she sparkles over the cool, calm waters of the ocean
Children are splashing happily, jumping over the white froth
> of the waves.

At night as she leaves the world, a blanket of stars takes her place.

Clare Cowley (15)
Elizabethan High School

AN ANGEL IN DISGUISE . . .

(Dedicated to my sister - Maddison-Amber Mary, born 12 July 1996)

Your sweet, scented breath,
Your star-spangled eyes,
The blessing of angels you carry inside,

Your soft, tender skin,
Your heart-warming smile,
The looks of an angel,
With jewels in your eyes,

Your kind, gentle heart,
Your young, cheerful mind,
The true colours of a rainbow,
You seek and you find,

Your vivid imagination,
So clear and unique,
Blue and pink mice,
Crowding whilst you sleep,

You reach out your hand,
And it touches my heart,
You fill me with love and with laughter,
My tiny sister, perfect from the start,
Your life will be happy ever after.

Hannah Jones (14)
Elizabethan High School

THE DOLL

She stands on my desk
Baby blue eyes staring
Rosebud mouth pouting
In scorn, she surveys her land
The room she has lived in
All her life
Like a queen
Or empress
She is an angel
Incapable of doing wrong
And yet
I feel a melancholy aura
I see sadness in those eyes
A longing for
Another world
But she is denied a release
She is trapped
And even her divine right
Cannot help her
Escape.

Natalie Bowen (14)
Elizabethan High School

AN AUTUMN DAY

On an autumn day I like walking to school.
The wind blows the branches on the trees,
The leaves on them clash together like clapping hands.

The whole world seems to be
Hibernating from the cruel weather,
Like prey hiding from its predator.

Like a million tiny diamonds is the dew on the grass,
As if it were part of the grounds of the Queen's palace,
On an almost emerald green carpet.

Leaves fall like rusty snowflakes,
Landing on the ground,
Creating a red carpet in front of me,
Awaiting my regal footsteps.

Leanne Dexter (14)
Elizabethan High School

SHOES

The high blue shoes stood proud in the shop
I could already feel the soft material wrapped around my feet
Like cotton cushioning my toes.
They are what feet were made for.
They smiled their cheesiest smile at passers-by.
They screamed at me 'Buy me' they said
How could I resist?

The shining lights in the shop window beamed down onto them.
I could feel the burning lights on my forehead like a bonfire.
They dominated the shop.
They passed contentedly in the window,
Humming, softly to everyone,
Oh I'll just go and try them on.

They fitted perfectly,
They felt as if they were heaven sent.
Like skin they clung to my feet,
They made people stop and stare.
'Go on, buy me,' they whispered,
So off I went with my brand new shoes.

Rachel Beth Groves (14)
Elizabethan High School

THE LION WHO HUNTED

The stripes of the zebras smudged together.
Curtains of black and white lay before the stealthy lioness.
Seas of tall grass camouflaged her from view
The zebras sniffed her musky scent.

The lioness sped on and hunted.
Hooves pounded on the dusty ground.
They cried out.
Fear made their nostrils
Flare with nervous excitement.
The muscles of the lioness rippled strongly as she sprinted on.

The strong zebras galloped by
Their eyes wide and bright.
The lioness jumped high in the humid air
Her claws dug into the leathery back of one of the herd.

The zebra collapsed in a heap on the dry grass.
The herd split up and ran apart,
As the zebra took its last painful breath.
The beige lioness had won its prize.

Vultures above in the cloudless sky
Screeched and gaped in awe
Waiting for their small share of the carcass.
Shadows cast upon the sand floor,
As they circled high in the bright blue sky.

The lioness had eaten her fill.
She stood on her powerful paws
And gracefully departed,
Head held high
And the vultures swooped down,
Fighting for every scrap.

Sheryl Earnshaw (14)
Elizabethan High School

BEAST OF THE NIGHT

The dull dark face full of horror,
Its body slimy, moist,
A panther in the moonlight,
A stalker of darkness,
Torturing cries crept through the air.

Beast exiled forever,
Prowler in the night,
A vision of satin,
Grinding his jaw,
The mayhem, massacre, moribund,
A hunter of you and me.

Chris Coyle (14)
Elizabethan High School

THE CHINA DOLL

She is so pretty with big blue eyes,
And she doesn't make any sound,
She doesn't move an arm or leg,
She is like a tiny mouse in a corner,
But bright like the sun in the sky.
Her bright teeth startle people walking past,
Speaking silently,
Paragraphs in her mind.

Michelle North (14)
Elizabethan High School

THE VOLCANO

A mountain of fear with a rumbling cough,
Sits and waits silently, stewing its lava.
The attractive exterior catches people's attention,
Until the time's run out.
Within an instant the ferocious beast comes to life.
Sparks of flames are blasted miles into the atmosphere,
Before settling silently into a mound of ash,
Leaving a quilt of eroded land.

Adele Brown (14)
Elizabethan High School

THE LOG

Silently sitting alone in a field of wasted dreams.
The haunting hollow log has a dark mysterious middle.
You never know what could be hiding in its curious centre.
The green glow of moss is flashed across the log's rim.
Roughened bark sits sharply waiting for its next victim.
The mossy smell gathers visitors in a hypnotic trance.

Heather Lloyd (14)
Elizabethan High School

A RIVER

The long meandering river flows softly down the hill,
The sides are worn away by time,
It is like the shape of a great long snake,
It is so powerful, there is nothing to stop it,
You can hear the water and it is so relaxing and comforting,
As it gradually reaches the top, it starts to run faster,
As it does so the water starts to make more noise,
It then twists, turns, topples and stops as it flows into the sea.

Claire Hales (14)
Elizabethan High School

THE GOALPOST

The old metallic goalposts
Stood shining in the sun,
While once sounds of many people
Screamed for that golden goal one.
But now they look so grim,
Rusted and no longer used
In a place that seems no fun.
'Til the council come next week
To erect another one.

Nathan Steen (14)
Elizabethan High School

THE CHINA CLOWN DOLL

The crooked white clown
Sits at the back of the cupboard,
Its face as pale as death,
The eyes as sharp as lightning,
Glowing green evil in the dark,
The whispers of wickedness,
Fill the darkness with fire,
Its shiny body is cracked with age,
Now the creaking cupboard closes
Yet its presence is still there, haunting . . .

Sophie Bryant (14)
Elizabethan High School

THE BOX

On the table sits an old bejewelled box,
The captor of dark secrets, long ago.
Grey cobwebs brush the roughened wooden case,
Where lace and silk-clad cuffs once rustled by.
Carved gargoyle faces rest within the wood,
Lit like small demons in the candlelight.
The haunting scent of cedar fills the room,
As sadly staring, emerald eyes look on.

Nyssa Walster (14)
Elizabethan High School

CRAZY GOLF

The windmill blocks the whole of hole number eight
It does its job well.
It stands there, in the middle of the rough carpet of hole number eight.
It's like a great big wooden flower spinning in the wind,
Its sails catching the breeze.
I hold the hard steel golf club in my hand,
Firmly ready to hit the small, round, illuminious rippled golf ball.
The smell of burgers and candyfloss waft with a tantalising smell,
Whilst the wooden windmill spins in the wind.

Shaun Roberts (14)
Elizabethan High School

FOOTBALL BOOTS

The enormous new boots
Had sharp, shiny studs
Like the ends of spears.
The colour was like the yolk of an egg.
The new boots spat at the other boots;
They were the best on the pitch.
When I ran, the boots whistled through the wind.

Luke Fagan (14)
Elizabethan High School

THE ROCK

The rock stands alone and cold,
With its jagged edges protruding into the sky.
The rock is like a guard,
He is a soldier standing to attention.
His colourful exterior overwhelms his onlookers.
He stands looking down on his admirers,
Smiling as they walk by.
The wind whistles wickedly through holes worn by time,
As he protects his land.

Michael Etchells (15)
Elizabethan High School

THE FOOTBALL

The football sits silently in the centre of the pitch,
Its white case crusty with mud,
Like a time-bomb waiting to explode,
Its bright shell waves to the onlooking fans,
There is a dull thud as the ball is kicked,
The ball is stroked around in a short simple style,
It seems to be glued to the players' feet.

James Kimberley (14)
Elizabethan High School

THE SKY

The deep blue ocean of wind
Surrounds me with beauty every day,
The separator of our world from the next.
The house of the gods.
Sometimes darkness falls and the gods are angry.
Destruction is caused.
The thrashing forks of lightning crash down
To finish the sins of the enemy.
The peace of the blue sky
Brings tranquillity back to its subjects.

Adam Kerley (14)
Elizabethan High School

THE WORLD

The world is at war
What can be done?
Can we save
What's left of us
People here
People there
People dead
Everywhere.
Will this be
The end of us?
Some suffer
Some don't.
What is expected of us all?
Some will die
Some will live
What will happen to those
Who do live?

Afia Amin (15)
Haywood School

SOCIETY

Pain, sorrow lives for today and lives for tomorrow
There's not a day goes by we don't shed a tear.
For family and friends we all have to fear
The streets are full of fear there's nowhere to turn
Where blood is shed there's a lesson to learn.
At the end of the story there's always a tail.
At the end of the day we never have to fail.
We fight for our rights in a different way
For tomorrow we live to see another day.

Sophia Rehman (15)
Haywood School

THE YOUTH OF TODAY

Why should we all have to suffer the pain
Of everyone playing their silly games?
Hurting whoever comes in their sight
They'll shout at them and start a fight
They shout, they yell, they scream and swear
They kick, they punch, they cause pain everywhere
Why should we let these people win?
We should wipe their face of their silly grin
And put a stop to their silly game
So no one else has to suffer the pain.

Emily Walton (14)
Haywood School

HER

Calmly she completed our final moments
Bringing our brief time together to a halt.
Hesitantly she gave out the warming smile which draws me in
Though on this occasion the effect is not achieved.
After a painful and uneasy pause I gazed into her eyes before
She slowly turned, walking away, leaving me, watching us
Becoming further and further apart.

I struggled through the rest of school somehow,
Never before have I been surrounded by so many friends
But felt so
Alone
And trapped within myself.
I could not bear to go home so soon that night
The day needed to last that little bit longer.
So instead, walking around the park in an attempt to gather myself,
The rough river shouting at me I move onto the trees where
Leaves and the wind together sing calm tunes to me
While the shadows hide me from the world's inquisitive view.

Sitting there I ponder how to return to my normal ways
But my now blank and empty mind distracts me from doing so.
From thinking of anything else as it's her that's filling me up,
Her softly spoken voice burning my ears.
Her name bruising my tired lips.
Her sweet hair fragrance attacking my nose.
Her I love.

Jacob Millin (16)
King Edward VI School

FIZZY CANDY

My sister Mandy loves fizzy candy
she says that it crackles in your mouth
I asked her where to get it
she said from a polar bear down South.

When I tried to make it crackle
it didn't work
my sister said 'You have to be
alone with the polar bear'
I've never really understood my sister Mandy
but I know she loves fizzy candy.

Ryan Willows (14)
King Edward VI School

THE OLD WOMAN

There was an old woman from Crete
Who liked to drink more than to eat.
So when she got near to a bottle of beer
She couldn't stand up on her feet.

There was an old woman from Crete
Who had a son that was called Pete.
And when he was home he was on the phone
Sat on a bale of wheat.

There was an old woman from Crete
Who had a dog that liked to eat.
His tail went round as he jumped up and down
Eating his big bowl of meat.

Louise Wilkinson (14)
King Edward VI School

24/7

Time swallows the future
and digests the past.
Time can catch up with us
we hardly notice how fast.
We have all the time in the world
to do so much more but
we can lose it unexpectedly
as if it had slipped quietly
out of a carelessly open door.
The world will keep on turning,
timing all our fates, so
do something right now
before you know it's too late.
Second after second.
Minute after minute.
Hour after hour.
The pendulum tocks
like an old rocking chair
to and fro it rocks.
Tick-tock, try to beat the clock.
Going on forever
until time itself says 'stop'.

Victoria Wyles (17)
King Edward VI School

A DREAMLIKE REALITY

Amongst the trees and grass and flowers
I saw a tiny shiny thing.
I tried to grab it, but it ran
And as it ran it began to sing.

What she sang, I did not know,
I tried to listen as best I could.
I asked her if she could repeat it,
And she politely replied that she would.

She sang of caves and dragons and fairies
Of wizards and witches and magical creatures.
All of them lived in her own special world,
Each of them had their own special features.

I asked her which world it was that she came from
Instead of an answer, she let out a scream.
The scream it shocked me, I didn't know why,
And then I awoke, it was only a dream.

Karla Barratt (16)
King Edward VI School

EQUINE

Liquid brown eyes, silken black hair
Proud and aloof, he always looks well groomed,
Challenging, sometimes cheeky.

Well-defined legs, dense hard muscles
He strides past, with a confidence all of his own
Domineering, almost dangerous.

A special relationship, shared between two
Someone to confide, who forgives my mistakes
Uncomplaining, never unloving
The equine.

Laura Baker (16)
King Edward VI School

Mum

Mum,
floating like a feather,
through the gentle breeze,
across the Scottish heather.

You're free now,
nothing to tie you down,
the world's your oyster,
you can go from town to town.

Over the ocean,
over the seas,
over the deserts,
with the cool gentle breeze.

Night sets in,
do I hear you sneeze?
No, you just carry on floating,
with the cool gentle breeze.

You can see all the sights,
you could never see before,
I lie here awake thinking of you,
just lying on the floor.

I'll never see you again,
as I understand,
not, anyway,
on this godforsaken land.

Gemma Burgess (16)
King Edward VI School

ALONE

We lie there, cold, freezing,
Our clothes rigid like a cardboard structure.
Guns ready, hearts scared, staring.
The mist stares back, we listen, but only
Silence, nothing.

The soft wind brought the sense of decaying bodies,
But we need not the wind as our minds see them.
I turn from the wind, I see the general turn, stone-cold
He blows, sharply, the signal, we charge.
Up we stand, shivering, scared, we run, we cross the

gap; bang, boom, crash, it started.
We ran as instructed, moving right then left, then left
like a robot but yet not.
I sense the danger, but feel nothing as I watch
friends fall, scream, die, staring at me.

My brother lies looking at me,
mouthing words, dying. Then, bang,
he pulled the trigger, he appeared motionful, but fell
splat on the floor, still staring as though awake.
I ran screaming, broke ranks, stumbled, fell, felt blood.

Blood, blood, it was me, my leg, my arm, my chest, then pain
my vision distorted as though my eyes were drunk, I think of home.
Home, it was fading, I saw not my wife but
blackness, blackness everywhere, yet nowhere. I start to move
I feel it, but stay motionless then.

David Gittins (16)
King Edward VI School

THE FUTURE

What does the future hold?

An alien encounter,
Robots which plan to rule the world,
Nuclear wars,
Medical advances,
Space travel to other planets,
Improved technology which will do anything we want,
But,
Who knows what the future holds,
In the new millennium?

Emma Foulds (16)
King Edward VI School

WHEN I'M GROWN UP . . .

This year I had a summer job
Looking after my little cousins.
Living with them.
I washed their hair, dried their tears.
When I was there
I realised, perhaps,
How hard I'd have to work
If I was a mum.
Without being paid
(No time off)
And I wondered
If I could do that
Am I overlooking the effort
For something I want, need?
Am I committed enough
(On top of a career)
To work for it?
Really work for it?
And is it worth it?

When I see my cousins smiling
Because of me
Kissing me, hugging me
Reaching for the safety of my hand.
It is.

Amy Law (15)
King Edward VI School

SURRENDER

I have surrendered to you again,
Once more your shadow falls across my life.
The little piece of resistance,
Has been dismissed,
By one bewitching smile.

All my problems are solved,
My pains are soothed,
And for one blissful moment,
I am happy.
Lost in the flow of your hair,
On a red summer evening,
Through the fields of golden corn,
And I know my ecstasy can never end,
Now that I have surrendered again.

But now it is the dark days of winter,
The reality of my situation hits me.
I am sapped of my strength,
By the harshness of the grey wasteland between us,
With only a faint glow,
For me to follow.

William Law (15)
King Edward VI School

MILLENNIUM

What does the millennium hold for me?
For me, for you, for us?
New technology, new advances, a brand new start.
But what about the wars?
What about the poverty?
Will we still be fighting or will we all be friends?
What does the millennium hold for me?
For me, for you, for us?

Sharon Walker (16)
King Edward VI School

AMONGST THE CROWD

Some of my friends are very different from me,
My friends will always mean a lot.
I want them to know, they're special,
They take away my tears,
And put a smile upon my face.
They always manage to make me laugh,
Each friend brings something new to me,
They complete my circle,
Some I see at school, others
I see once a week and some I haven't met yet,
But I want them all to know,
'Thank you'
But most of all to tell a certain few,
That have always been there,
And hopefully will stay,
How much I appreciate and value them.

Elaine Chambers (15)
King Edward VI School

DUELLING DRAGONS

As we walk towards their lairs,
Our hearts miss a beat, our legs start to quiver,
The excitement starts to build,
Are we mad or are we sane?

The walk is long towards our fate,
The surroundings tell us the story of battle,
The ice that froze, the fire that burnt,
Which to choose we will soon decide.

In the dark we near the end,
Cold to the right, heat to the left,
The adrenaline runs as we make our choice,
We choose ice and pray that we're right.

We mount the raging beast;
Higher and higher he goes,
He's preparing for battle,
All we can do is wait.

Then with amazing speed the battle begins,
We twist and turn, thrown without mercy,
We glimpse the creature called fire,
They interweave with astonishing skill.

The screams now loud pierce the air,
Anticipated collisions vanish in seconds,
The movements are swift,
As we soar through the sky.

As the speed decreases it comes to an end,
A feeling of thrill has replaced our nerves,
We have survived and the dragon has come to no harm,
We leave as the dragon prepares to fight again.

James Renshaw (15)
King Edward VI School

A PLANET BEYOND THE SKY

We parted daylights ago,
Over feelings I didn't show,
But now that girl has gone,
And a new one has become.

So go to your window and see,
The present that is given to you from me.

I give you the moon because like my heart,
It shows how two lovers were torn apart,
So far away and precious, positioned in the sky,
Treat it with respect, it's not for you to buy.

It seems impossible to land upon,
One night it's there and then it's gone,
But the few that do will see,
Just how beautiful and special it can really be.

Look at the moon and see,
That you'll always be watched over by me,
You may be confused about what to do,
But I know that I'm still in love with you.

I know I didn't give you the world,
But I was just a girl,
And just as the Earth isn't complete without the moon,
I've a star missing too but I hope it will reappear soon.

Vicki Perkins (16)
King Edward VI School

CIGARETTE

On the golden beach you were sat,
With the poison draining into your soul.
I was jealous, where was it going?
Desperately I wanted to follow.

So close to your mouth it lingered there,
The ideal place I wish I was near.
Every breath and intake of the poison,
I felt it could be myself getting closer.

The waves of love had left my shore,
And the burning of poison was getting further
How can something be so invert,
Why can't it be me?

Please stub it out and throw away,
But don't mourn over the ashes,
You don't need that putrid flavour,
Take a taste of me!

Michelle Hancock (16)
King Edward VI School

LOVE IN THE OCEAN

I wake up in the morning
And you have already left
You set sail across the ocean
And left lying in bed

The sea is coming in
And the waves are crashing harder
The anchors strain under the tension
Trying to stay a grip

I thought by now
Things would have changed
But your unpredictable pattern
Is starting to irritate me

It's time for both of us to depart
And leave this harbour
For other ports
Good night. Safe trip.

Helen Clewes (16)
King Edward VI School

THE SEA OF LOVE

A new tide crawls carefully in.
Sun shining onto the blue and green surface;
Creating thousands of sparkling diamonds.
Slowly tempting you to enter its vast and inviting ocean.
Beautiful to look at, calm, fun, exciting, unpredictable.

As you curiously enter the intriguing ocean,
You are enclosed by its waves,
All you can see for miles is the ocean,
It's just you and the ocean.

The water twinkles with the sun, inviting you in deeper,
The further in you go, the safer and more confident you feel,
As you begin to grow comfortable with the waves wrapping
Themselves around you, hugging you, needing you, loving you.

You want it to last forever,
But the tide begins to turn,
Slowly the waves unwrap themselves from around you,
The current gets weaker and you are no longer a part
Of this immense ocean.

The last trickle of water from around your ankles is
Pulled back into the huge blueness,
Leaving you lonely on the wet sand as it travels
Further and further away until it's just a distant memory.

You had entered the sea of love.

Rebecca Osborn (16)
King Edward VI School

STARRY NIGHT

Alone at night, only one star in sight.
The tiny glow away from arm's reach,
drawing closer, closer, nearer to me each day.
The star alight, burning with desire.
Fiery head, flame in the heart.
At one together not knowing we may drift apart.
Feeding from each other whenever we meet.
Security beneath your glow.
Treasuring you, always close to my heart.
The fuel disappearing, no more light to see.
Not even a tiny glow flickering in the sea.
No more glowing for me.

Lindsey Hull (16)
King Edward VI School

LOVE IS LIKE RAIN

Storm brews, rain pours.
Sometimes it's a sudden downpour of sadness
Sometimes it's a pitter-patter of happiness.

Rain.

Often it's not wanted but it still pours.
Grey, dull, black,
Scared, terrified, mad.

Rain.

It rains on the outside,
But seeps into the heart,
Dampening and destroying.

Rain.

Rain, rain, go away,
Please don't come back
Any day.

Sarah Brammer (16)
King Edward VI School

A RED BALLOON

Love is a helium balloon, red and new and bright,
Held close to your chest with all your might,
And in one second something tugs at the strings
And suddenly she is free, testing her new-found wings.

She is up with the birds in the clear, blue sky,
And now she has love she's naturally high.
Riding the wind, she has her head in the clouds,
Regardless of people, noises and sounds.

People beneath her all wonder and stare
But she is oblivious and doesn't care.
They all see her but she doesn't see them,
All she notices is one of the men.

She feels light-headed as she floats over the town,
She is carefree and happy and doesn't look down,
Because if she did, she'd know she's heading for a fall,
And that one short sharp stab to the heart could end it all.

One unexpected mistake and the balloon would go pop,
The love would escape and her heart would then drop.
The powerful chemical, that one called love,
Has been taken away from up above.

She can feel herself shrivelling and dropping to the floor,
And all because she has no love anymore.
No love to uplift her and take her to the sky
Instead she keeps falling and feels herself die.

Melissa Highfield (16)
King Edward VI School

HER THOUGHT

She doesn't seem to be focused
On who she is anymore.
She's lost her way
On a long winding road.
She's been possessed by infatuation.
She's bewildered by her
Hopes and dreams.
Her mind knows only one thing
Her only desire.
I see her in my mind's eye
Sitting, lost in thought, of a thought.
A singular concept has gradually
Taken over her life.

Annie Bethell (16)
King Edward VI School

THE LIFE OF A MATCH

A match shining bright in darkness,
One bright soul showing the way for others,
But this shining light soon fades away,
And once again, I'm trapped in darkness.

A match is a simple thing,
But from one little match,
So much hope can be found,
This match can see into the future,
And bring me so much more in life.

The match is slowly dying,
It is gradually fading away,
No longer can I see into the future,
Or hope for so much in life.

The match has now died
Useless now.
Just a piece of burned out wood,
Which brings me no light,
Or any hope in my life.

Claire Waller (16)
King Edward VI School

ODE TO THE HUMMING BIRD

With a wing beat thousands of times an hour,
She hums as she hovers in front of the flower.
Her beak, so delicate, long and thin,
To steal the treasure from within,
For existence it is nature's duty,
So created was this bird of beauty.
Unique with the gift of motionless flight,
She can work through the day and sleep through the night.
In the haze of the forest a song can be heard,
The glorious tune of the humming bird.

Helena Cherrill (15)
King Edward VI School

WHO WANTS TO BE A MILLIONAIRE?

20 million people glued to their televisions
The familiar theme tune ends
It is time.
Chris Tarrant waits patiently for an answer
'Final answer? . . . Sure? . . . Positive?
Not A? . . . Not B? . . . Not C?
Well, you had £32,000 . . .
We'll take a break!'
Oh dear! The contestant's nerves are stretched to the limit!
'Hmmm . . . maybe I should've asked the audience . . . .
Or phoned Charlie? Oh damn!
He would've known!'
Then Chris Tarrant is back again
'Well, I *can* tell you that it's the . . .
Wrong answer!'
Then the process begins all over again.
Mind you, it can't be too bad,
Not if it's one of the most popular shows ever,
But will anyone *ever* win the £1 million prize?
I wonder . . .

James Waite (15)
King Edward VI School

WHY?

The world is changing me.
I'm spiralling into the dank, dingy world below.
I'm like a butterfly with only one wing, struggling to fly.
I'm not sure where I belong anymore.
The mental confusion I feel, is pulling me down.
I reach up to the top but my hand just crumbles the rubble.
I'm clinging on with all my might . . .
But I'm just falling into nothing . . .

Why?

Olivia Crampton (15)
King Edward VI School

2020

Just imagine

There are no trees left in our once beautiful forest.
There are no small delicate flowers breaking through the earth.
There are no birds singing in the morning, just a deadly silence.
All the countryside and its animals have disappeared.

There are no reefs full of life.
There are no sea creatures splashing in the once cool, clean water.
There are no whales and dolphins playing in a ship's wake.
All that remains is a vast expanse of dirty, polluted water.

There's nothing of any worth left in this world,
Just sky rise building after sky rise building.
Our once beautiful land and sea no longer exists.
The Earth's future is no longer secure.

Ella Pearson (15)
King Edward VI School

RAIN BALLAD

When I woke up I thought what a day
Outside it was cold and the sky was grey
It went dark and the rain came down
Faster and faster onto the ground.

I went to the shop down the street
Puddles appeared in front of my feet
As I walked down the slippery wet road
All I wanted was to be home.

I got back home and was very glad
Then I looked out the window and felt sad
When the weather is humble so is my mood
I wish it'd go sunny real soon.

Then I heard thunder and saw a flash of light
The clouds were gone and it looked like night
On the streets it started to flood
If I could change the weather I would.

Samantha Utting (14)
Kirkby Centre

MOON DUSK
(The Eclipse)

D ark shadows lengthen
   All eyes gaze
   At the spectacle
   Amidst the haze

U mbra falls
   The world is still
   As the deathly hush engulfs us
   The corona glows

S ilence is broken
   As the diamond ring appears
   People gasp, mouth agape
   Day begins again

K ind Druids dance
   And make a scene
   The air is filled with life
   Three bounds to the right
   Two to the left
   This is the dance
   The dance of a lifetime.

Andrea Stott (14)
Minster School

OLD OR YOUNG?

She stands as if a statue.
Her purpose is unknown,
Her clothes are but rags,
And patches have been sewn

To hide gaping holes,
Where sunkist skin peeps.
Her face is deeply shadowed,
Where the essence of age creeps

Hiding her unknown beauty,
Caressing her untimely soft skin,
Chasing away her sparkle,
Hiding her masculine grin

That once dazzled strangers
But filled them with rage.
The days of great living are over
As she is consumed with age.

Jenna Hogan (14)
Orchard School

THE WORLD OF PEACE

Look deep and imagine
You are in a world where the oceans are shallow
Even a man can touch the base
Look deep and imagine
You could see the end of the world on the horizon
This world is flat

The stars are the descendants of the past
Look deep
And just imagine a world where the people talk
And the people mix
There's no war on their mind, these nations of peace
No war! No war!

Imagine no war
There are those in our world fighting for homes
And for trees
People starving and yet others throw food away

The nations fight for the unknown
So what is the world like, ask yourself?

This world will have no life, after one big war

Just think of the little children dying
Under the oath of war!
Their religions and origin the question?

Just imagine their parents on a train, on their way to get a bullet
The ones that ran and got caught were hung under the silent tree

In this world God is locked away, and the Devil is left to roam

In my world where I look deep
The people share what they have and look after the others
And the doves fly free

Remember this world can be free
If you and I change our ways
Peace can be there, peace can be there.

Matt Hayton (15)
Orchard School

LOVE-HATE

With you, my friend
I don't know what to do
I've got a love-hate relationship
Like lies against what's true.

Sometimes you're crazy
You upset me more than you know.
Other times I love you,
On me you tend to grow.

Look below what's on the surface
See what lies under
Never fear, I'll be here
I will never sunder.

Forget all emotions
To me all I have is two
Love and hate relationships
Between me and you.

Christopher Stokes (14)
Orchard School